THE ECCENTRICS

© 2016 Assouline Publishing
3 Park Avenue, 27th floor
New York, NY 10001 USA
Tel.: 212-989-6769 Fax: 212-647-0005
www.assouline.com

Art direction: Camille Dubois
Editorial direction: Esther Kremer
Printed in Canada.
ISBN: 9781614285816

THE ECCENTRICS

PHOTOGRAPHS *by* RUVEN AFANADOR

TEXT *by* HAL RUBENSTEIN

ASSOULINE

The poor are crazy; the rich eccentric.

Introduction *6*

Dita Von Teese *8*

Iris Apfel *16*

Lauren Ezersky *24*

Donna Karan *32*

Douglas Little &
Jodi Lyn O'Keefe *38*

Edward Bess *48*

Erin Wasson *54*

Kelly Wearstler *62*

Patrick McDonald *68*

Lynn Yaeger *74*

INTRODUCTION
TO THE ECCENTRICS

The funny thing about people who possess singular gifts or galvanizing eccentricities is that they often aren't quite sure why we're making such a fuss about them. Their world is in a parallel universe, spinning on a different axis, affording views of the same objects, opportunities, and people we see that are heightened, zoom-lensed, and frequently skewed. The powers derived from these perspectives are launched when hesitancy and comparison to conventional wisdom is discarded, their idiosyncrasy is embraced as the norm, and not only are they sticking to it, they can't wait to build new realities around it.

Eccentrics do know they are different, if only because we keep telling them they are and they see our wide-eyed reaction to their ceaseless capacity to curate and nurture beauty unearthed from unexpected corners. But questioning why they are "that way" or how they "do it" is a pointless endeavor. However, learning what stimulus makes them come alive, discerning the determination that often matches or even supersedes their ability, and exploring what exterior forces shaped them, who they are grateful for, and what they dream of does prove enlightening.

To celebrate the opening of the new Forty Five Ten, a store created to showcase the wonders wrought by eccentric talent and now reimagined as a vast, stunning space where such singularity can thrive in abundance, co-founder Brian Bolke has commissioned photographer Ruven Afanador and myself to spotlight, provoke, and ultimately engage eleven exceptional and disparate men and women—artists, designers, performers, creators, writers, and a couple who simply are their own parade. Each of them has established residency on this alternative axis in order to cultivate, refine and eagerly share their vision of an existence where beauty is fluid, imaginative design is equally celebrated for its function, seduction is possible and encouraged at any age, reinvention and surprise have no expiration date and where trusting in one's individuality can result in more magic than any genie popping out of a bottle. But what ultimately makes eccentrics so enthralling and enviable is that their norm is rooted in a fervent desire to use what they've learned to make today special, and their eagerness to discover what could make tomorrow an even better day. And that's what all the fuss is about.

Hal Rubenstein

$\mathcal{N}^{\underline{o}}1$

Dita Von Teese

HER PERSONA IS THE EXPONENTIAL OF ARTIFICE, A STUDIED REALIZATION OF THE IDEALIZED FEMALE, THE RESULT OF A DAZZLED AND DAZZLING IMAGINATION THAT HAS CHERRY-PICKED FAVORITE TRAITS OF HOLLYWOOD SIRENS FROM ITS GOLDEN AGE, WORLD WAR II PIN-UP GIRLS, PLAYBOY MAGAZINE WHEN IT MATTERED, AND INDOMITABLE, CORSETED SEDUCTRESSES OF BURLESQUE'S HEYDAY LIKE SALLY RAND AND LILI ST. CYR. WHAT MAKES HER PRESENCE SO EXTRAORDINARY IS NOT MERELY HER BEAUTY, HER TALENT, OR HER WINKING CHARM. IT'S THAT SHE THRUST THIS OBSESSION WITH A FORGOTTEN AND DISMISSED ART FORM SOLELY ON HER OWN. SHE DIDN'T CATCH A WAVE. SHE WASN'T DISCOVERED. SHE MADE THIS HAPPEN, APPEARING ON STAGE AS A PORCELAIN GODDESS IN A GIANT MARTINI GLASS, DARING US TO TAKE A SIP. AND WE'VE BEEN DRUNK ON HER EVER SINCE.

HAL RUBENSTEIN: I've always been struck by the single-mindedness of your obsession.

DITA VON TEESE: I always wanted to be this way, even when I was young. All my fantasies were about imagining who I might become. Other people look back on their childhood as some magical period. I couldn't wait to grow up and pick out my own clothes.

HR: Nevertheless, this is not a dream that could be realized as a child. When did you start acting on it?

DVT: When I was twelve, I wasn't advanced like other girls my age. I was shy. I wanted to take ballet classes and read books, not the stuff for winning a lot of popularity contests. I think people started noticing me at nineteen or twenty, when I started dressing up with red lipstick and long red nails, dying my hair black, and applying cat-eye eyeliner, inspired by World War II pin-up girls, many of whom were also burlesque dancers. Suddenly, I had a more powerful persona. When I realized people felt a little intimidated by me, I said, "Wow this stuff can give you power."

HR: Were you hoping to be discovered like Lana Turner and wind up in the movies?

DVT: No, I didn't see it as a stepping-stone to becoming an actress or recording star. My reason was simple. I have always wanted to be the best burlesque star in the world. This was always my mission even though it wasn't popular at the time.

HR: Other people have adopted what one might call retro glamour.

DVT: Of course, many people have tried on a look like mine. The difference is, my kind of style is a place most people visit but rarely stay. At first they think it's cool, but then they start feeling restricted,

...my kind of style is a place most people visit but rarely stay. But this is my reality.

or think it's fussy, or they get a boyfriend who doesn't get off on the look, or they move on to the next big thing. But this is my reality.

HR: How did you manage to revive burlesque?

DVT: I started doing shows in strip and fetish clubs. I pushed my way in. My breakthrough probably came at The Torture Garden, a famous fetish club in the UK. It was the first time a club of this sort staged a burlesque event. Some asked what's fetishistic about burlesque, but others ate it up. Then I performed with the Pussycat Dolls at a series of shows in Hollywood at the Roxy and got singled out for the martini glass number. I did *Playboy* and performed at the Mansion when it was still a big deal. It wasn't overnight. It was little by little. Marc Jacobs hired me for a big Louis Vuitton opening. That led to being the first American headliner at the Crazy Horse in Paris. That was major.

HR: Can this be a lifelong career?

DVT: Three years ago I decided to slow down and retire, but I got asked to perform at the Crazy Horse again. I hesitated because those girls who work there are so young. I worried how I would measure up. But we sold out 8,000 tickets, they wrote that I was better than ever, and the girls were like "Can you teach me how you do this?"

HR: What did you take from that?

DVT: Age doesn't really matter. One of the goals of my new show Strip Strip Hooray is to show beauty at all stages of life. I was foolish to be afraid I wouldn't be at my best. When you're young you can't even understand how an older woman could steal your man away. But you do get sexier as you get older if you believe in yourself. I have

always been interested in the women who became notorious, who thrived through a cultivation of erotic wit and wisdom.

HR: What do you wear offstage?

DVT: I am a big fan of fifties dresses and ballet flats. I have a high maintenance look, and what I love about a dress is the ease. There are less seams and fabric to bind you. Dresses give you freedom. Otherwise, who has time to pick out all those "cute" looks?

HR: You never wear jeans and a T-shirt?

DVT: I do on Halloween. My girlfriends think it's hilarious. I get a spray tan and beige nails, lips and toenails. No one recognizes me. At first it's fun. But I also lose all my VIP privileges and very strange men try to talk to me. I can't wait to wash off the beige.

Iris
APFEL

"How are you, beautiful lady?"

ASKS A BEAMING PASSERBY ON OUR RIGHT AS I ESCORT THE OBJECT OF HER AFFECTION INTO HER PARK AVENUE ADDRESS. ON OUR LEFT IS ANOTHER YOUNGER WOMAN, BLUSHING AS SHE MOUTHS THE WORDS, "SHE'S JUST WONDERFUL, ISN'T SHE?" HOW MANY HUMANS DO YOU KNOW WHO EXUDE INCOMPARABLE STYLE AT ANY AGE, LET ALONE THIS WOMAN WHO SHAMES NEARLY EVERYONE FROM ANY ERA WITH HER EFFORTLESS AND IRRESISTIBLE PANACHE. POP CULTURE'S CURRENT VENERATED "IT GIRL" MAY ALSO BE ITS SHARPEST AND BUSIEST (A LIST OF HER PROJECTS IN DEVELOPMENT COULD SEND A TYPE-A EVP OF EITHER SEX ONTO A THERAPIST'S COUCH BEMOANING HIS/ HER LIFE AS A SLACKER) AS WELL AS ITS MOST TRENCHANT OBSERVER. BEHOLD THIS BORN STORYTELLER'S OFF-THE- BAKELITE-CUFF MINI MASTER CLASS.

HAL RUBENSTEIN: If it isn't New York's hottest snow-cropped babe!

IRIS APFEL: I know. It's insane. At my stage of the game I should be out to pasture instead of being a 94-year-old cover girl. I'm really very flattered, though everyone asking to take selfies with me is driving me insane.

HR: What did you do to cause this, Iris?

IA: I haven't a clue. But America is on a big search. People are realizing they need something better than this celebrity culture we have created with its pretty dreadful role models. They aren't inspirational. How can you live vicariously through the Internet, like so many try to do, when there isn't any glamour or curiosity to it? You can't acquire soul through lip service. You have to live it and invest in it.

HR: It doesn't sound like you envy today's youth.

IA: No, I love them. They are so talented and eager, but I'm glad I'm not young anymore, because they've been programmed to be in such a rush. But you can't get everything by pressing a button. You have to cultivate the parts of life you want to excel in, enjoy, and keep. It's like having a beautiful voice but never practicing. You'll sing, but you will never become an artist. Anything worth doing is worth putting the time in.

HR: How did you acquire your singular style?

IA: I didn't acquire it. I had it. It's either in your DNA or it's not. Fashion you can buy, but style you must possess. That said, just because you may have it doesn't mean you know what to do with it. It still must be nurtured and trusted.

HR: So how did you do that?

IA: I was handed a memorable life lesson from Mrs. Loehmann, the legendary discount retailer. I lived in Astoria, Queens, and usually stayed close to home, but one day I got turned around on the subway and wound up on Bedford Avenue in Brooklyn, where I came upon this shop window with a handsome Tiffany glass screen and a mannequin wearing a Norell. And by the way, people should know Norell isn't a perfume. He was a great American designer. Anyone who says they love fashion should look him up and study his work because it was so glamorous; you really must.

Anyway, I go in the store and it's bedlam, with lots of women running around in various stages of undress and disgruntled husbands tapping their feet, all surrounded by a lot of cheap junk jammed onto pipe racks. Meanwhile, where is this Norell? Then I learn that you have to go to Loehmann's back room. Finally, I find it, open the door, and it's like walking into Aladdin's cave, full of Pauline Trigeres (another designer everyone should know), Mort Zuckermans, and Norells at prices I never thought I could aspire to own.

Well, I started making pilgrimages to Loehmann's. And I keep noticing this woman who looks like something out of Toulouse-Lautrec. She even has a 19th-century high-neck blouse and skirt to the floor. She may even have worn high-button shoes and her hair in a topknot. And she'd sit taking in the room like she was watching a tennis match, except the last few times I realized she had fixated on me, and it made me very uncomfortable. So I acknowledged her stares and she came over to me. "I watch you every time you come in," Mrs. Loehmann said. "Don't let anyone ever tell you that you are beautiful, because you are not. But you have style, real style, and that is worth far more. Don't forget it. Ever."

HR: Did her comments rattle you?

IA: I forgot about what she said almost instantly. I was too busy getting my bargains. But over time I understood what she meant. Style isn't anything cerebral. It's all from the gut: instinct coupled with desire.

HR: So do you apply the mantra when you get dressed each day?

IA: No. I don't think much about getting dressed at all. Once you trust it, you don't have to. In fact, I am always in a hurry. But I have my favorite pieces like this Scandinavian wood necklace handy, or a stunning lacquer red/orange velvet Trigere cape that I paid thirty-five-dollars for at Loehmann's years ago. You cannot believe the quality. In fact, quality is everything when you shop, not price. I love a bargain, but it's only a bargain when the merchandise is superior. I don't throw quality clothes away, though I sometimes turn the fabrics into pillows.

HR: See, this is what the Internet needs. You should do an advice column.

IA: Oh, no. People ask me too many personal questions now as it is. And God save me from bloggers. I told you, people have to stop going online and go get themselves a life. So far, I've quite enjoyed having one.

You have to cultivate the parts of life you want to excel in, enjoy, and keep. It's like having a beautiful voice but never practicing.

N.º 3

Lauren Ezersky

NOT THAT SHE DIDN'T WORK, BUT SHE WAS ONE OF THE FIRST PEOPLE I EVER KNEW IN NEW YORK WHO WAS CELEBRATED FOR BEING CELEBRATED, AND SHE DID IT LONG BEFORE YOU COULD ACHIEVE THIS SIMPLY BY POSTING A SHOT OF YOURSELF EVERY TIME YOU LEFT THE HOUSE, PRETENDED YOU WERE HAVING FUN, OR PUT A HAT ON YOUR POOR EXPLOITED DOG. SHE IS PROOF THAT NOTABLE STYLE IS NOT ABOUT TAKING ENDLESS RANDOM PICTURES. IT'S ABOUT TAKING STOCK OF WHAT SETS YOU APART FROM EVERYONE ELSE AND REALIZING YOU REALLY LIKE THE PERSON YOU DISCOVERED.

HAL RUBENSTEIN: I've known you forever, and you've always looked and dressed exactly this way.

LAUREN EZERSKY: Hey, I don't think I'm eccentric, but everyone else does. Okay, I know I'm not normal looking, whatever normal may be, who knows, but I've always worn tons of makeup and worn whatever I wanted.

HR: Did you ever feel you had to dress more like a fashion editor?

LE: No, because they don't dress that stylishly. The fun of loving fashion for its own sake is that it gives you the freedom to put on a ball gown to go to the supermarket or wear jeans to a black-tie event. Unfortunately, the options aren't what they used to be, so it's a little harder to have fun.

HR: Why?

LE: Nobody dresses up anymore. To be photographed, maybe, and get more followers, but not really to actually go do anything. People and companies aren't spending like they used to, to produce the kind of nights where you can really turn it out.

HR: Was standing out always second nature?

LE: I guess. When I was growing up, you opened a magazine and saw Cheryl Tiegs and Christie Brinkley, and I sure didn't look like them. I had long dark hair. I was skinny. I didn't have a tiny cheerleader nose. With no one to aspire to, I dressed the way I liked at school. I got sent to the office a lot. I'd wear high red, white, and blue socks with a really short skirt, or I'd wear multicolored fishnets that I bought at some cheesy department store.

HL: So you never dressed conservatively?

LE: I wore a uniform once—black pants, white shirt, and bow tie—when I was the relish girl at Cooky's Steak Pub on Central Avenue in Yonkers. But I worked there because there were these shoes I wanted at Thom McAn. They were eighty-nine dollars—a lot of money in those days—for these brogues with a chunky heel that my mother took one look at and couldn't believe I wasted money on them. Little did she know what Manolos would cost.

HR: Was getting a job in fashion easier or harder because of your individuality?

LE: I knew no one. So I went to 1411 Broadway, the big office building in the garment center, and went floor-to-floor, office-to-office, asking for work. I got a job as a receptionist, then in showroom sales, then as a buyer. Then I became my own boss selling jewelry in the garment center, then to designers, well, more like people who worked for designers, like Halston and Donna and Geoffrey Beene. And while they were buying, I asked them to get me into shows. It wasn't about skill. It was about assertiveness. I've never taken no or a turndown personally.

HR: When did you finally get some traction or recognition?

LE: A girlfriend of mine who was a producer for Oprah Winfrey got me on that show for being a shopaholic. That led to booking an appearance on the early fashion cable show called *Behind the Velvet Ropes*, but the interviewer stomped off the set right before airtime, so when they panicked for a replacement I said, "I'm right here." And I stayed. The Style Channel eventually picked up the show, and then Moët & Chandon bought in. That was a big deal because no one was making money on TV doing fashion back then. You did it because you loved it.

Okay, I know I'm not normal looking, whatever normal may be, who knows...

HL: What does this shopaholic love to buy?

LE: Jewelry and coats. Anything by Alaia, Galliano and Prada, well, old Prada. But then I love vintage, both clothes and jewelry. I hit 47th Street—the diamond district in Manhattan—but I know what I'm looking for.

HR: What are some of your favorite pieces?

LE: My diamond Chopard watch, my Chrome Hearts leather jacket, and a dress by John Bates, a designer who did Emma Peel's (Diana Rigg) clothes in the original *The Avengers* TV show in the mid-60s. I don't think I've worn it in thirty years, but I paid $500 for it, and it is amazing.

HR: Do people dress with more or less individuality than they used to?

LE: There are more affordable places to shop so there's so much stuff available, but it doesn't matter if you don't figure out who you are. The Internet is full of people who keep asking for someone else's validation. And that's sad. I say make an effort. Trust your instincts. Fall in love with makeup because it lets you be who you want to be. Don't buy only labels. Tahari can be fabulous if you know what you are doing. And if you make a mistake, who gives a shit? You'll wear something different tomorrow.

HR: If you could dress like anyone in the movies, real life or fiction, which person would it be?

LE: Cruella de Vil. I didn't much like her attitude about the puppies, but man, all that black and white with the red lipstick! She's fierce.

Donna Karan

SHE, RALPH AND CALVIN WILL FOREVER BE THE TRIUMVIRATE OF AMERICAN FASHION. HER INITIALS ARE HALF OF THE MOST RECOGNIZABLE ABBREVIATION IN THE ANNALS OF BRANDING, WITH DKNY PERMANENTLY FUSING THE DESIGNER'S NAME, ENERGY AND AESTHETIC WITH HER BELOVED HOMETOWN.

AND YET, THE CREATOR OF THE WARDROBE-CHANGING "7 EASY PIECES" HAS EQUALLY RELISHED HER TWO LONGSTANDING UNOFFICIAL PART-TIME GIGS. HER FIRST IS AS 7TH AVENUE'S ANGEL OF MERCY, RALLYING COLLEAGUES TO GIVE BACK TO FIGHT AIDS (7TH ON SIXTH), OVARIAN CANCER (SUPER SATURDAY), PEDIATRIC AIDS (KIDS 4 KIDS) OR HELPING HAITIANS REBOUND RISE UP AFTER THE DEVASTATING 2010 EARTHQUAKE.

HER OTHER SELF-APPOINTED MISSION IS AS FASHION'S REIGNING PAIN IN THE BUTT, FOREVER RAILING AGAINST THE DISJOINTED TIMING OF RUNWAY SHOWS, DELIVERIES, AND THE SURFEIT OF MERCHANDISE WHILE PREACHING FOR THE INCORPORATION OF SUSTAINABILITY, WELLNESS, AND INDIGENOUS GLOBAL CRAFTSMANSHIP, USING HER LINE, URBAN ZEN, AS EXHIBIT A.

UNTIL RECENTLY, HER MANTRAS WERE MET WITH "OH, THAT'S JUST DONNA." SUDDENLY, THE INDUSTRY IS REALIZING THE BLACK CASHMERED CASSANDRA OF AMERICAN RETAIL WASN'T MERELY RANTING. SHE WAS RIGHT ALL ALONG. NO WONDER, AFTER FOUR DECADES, SHE STILL FEELS LIKE A CRUSADING OUTSIDER.

HAL RUBENSTEIN: So, you want to start off with a big "I told you so!"

DONNA KARAN: Not yet. There's some movement at Burberry and Tom Ford, and there's an awful lot of hand wringing, but how long have I been talking about in-season showing, in-season dressing, and buy-now-wear-now, yet the Europeans and too many others still don't get it.

HR: What don't they get?

DK: They are confusing the customer. No, they are pissing her off, and it's killing the industry.

HR: How?

DK: It was different when you didn't see the clothes if you weren't at a runway show until they showed up in a magazine or a store. They are all over the Internet now instantly, but you still can't buy them and by the time you can, you've seen them too many times to care, plus Zara has probably already knocked them off. Good for Zara.

HR: But isn't that going to happen with Urban Zen?

DK: Nope. I'm putting out only what's in season. I'm not posting it early. I'm avoiding silk dresses in August. I'm avoiding big stores. Actually, I love my marketplace so far. We'll expand, but slowly. I know eventually we have to make money, but after four decades on Seventh Avenue, I'm enjoying starting over again.

HR: But you are starting up in a very different world.

DK: I have a lot of sympathy for young designers, and not just because it's such a challenging time right now. When Calvin, Ralph, and I took off, Europe and being global didn't matter. We could create for and build our own community. Other countries nurtured designers that reflected their own region. There was such diversity

of product. We didn't produce six collections a year plus diffusion lines. We had the time to experiment, explore, to be inspired. Now young designers must be everywhere immediately, ship new, new, new every six weeks, and face buyers who choose the same six colors regardless of who is designing. That's why everything looks the same in the stores. It's numbing.

HR: Then how do you get your blood flowing?

DK: Nature. Look, I know you tease me, but I do talk to the sky, rocks, and trees when I go out to my house in the Hamptons or in Parrot Cay. They reveal fresh colors, shapes, and textures. And then there is Haiti and Bali. I have always believed in conscious consumerism, putting worlds together so people discover that style isn't just about clothes. It's about devising a positive environment from beyond what you know, filling it with artisan handcrafts and furniture made by loving families who are often happier with simple things in life than people living with abundance in big cities. Every time I bring people to Haiti they are blown away.

HR: Is New York no longer the apple of your eye, so to speak?

DK: Look, I am a New Yorker tried and true, a workaholic like everyone else, never satisfied like everyone else. Always wanting more. But when I leave New York now, I see that more isn't necessarily what I thought it was. "More" may be about calm, health, meditation, comfort, yoga, and previously unexplored places, like New Guinea or Tibet. I don't think 'more' can be gotten online. It's to be found in your heart and your soul, and in reaching out to and getting back from others. This focus on comfort, kindness, and craft is what I am trying to incorporate in Urban Zen. The clothes should just be one part of a bigger landscape. It's a lot to put out there, but I want to try, even if it means incorporating more non-urban influences. Who knows? Maybe all the clothes we sell won't be black.

Douglas Little & Jodi Lyn O'Keefe

THEY DON'T LOOK MADE FOR EACH OTHER, BUT AS BOTH
EAGERLY POINT OUT, LOOKS ARE OFTEN MEANT TO BE
DECEIVING. THEY'VE ONLY BEEN A COUPLE FOR SLIGHTLY
OVER A YEAR, BUT AS NEITHER IS UNDERSTATED IN LOOK OR
MOOD, THEY RADIATE THE MAKINGS OF AN EPIC ROMANCE,
GOTHIC AND DARK BY CHOICE, YET DEVOID OF DEMONS. THINK
WUTHERING HEIGHTS WITH A VERY HAPPY ENDING.

I realized the punkest thing I could do was acquire manners, cultivate being a gentleman, being kind, and writing thank you notes.

HAL RUBENSTEIN: When were you tipped off that you weren't like the other kids?

DOUGLAS LITTLE: I was "chosen" at an early age. Being born a redhead automatically makes you an outsider, thanks to all those myths and assumptions about "gingers." But rather than get angry about it, I thought, why not embrace it? So I never had any intention of blending in, quickly deciding to see the world through my own vision.

JODI LYN O'KEEFE: As soon as I came to L.A. as a teenager to work in television, it was pretty obvious. I have dark hair. I love a red lip. I avoid the sun. I look gothic and harsh. Not very beachy.

HR: How did your physical traits affect your artistic endeavors?

DL: I instinctively began looking for beauty in the unusual, the dark, and the strange. Now, what's strange depends on your point of view. When I was thirteen, I became an avid punk rocker, but then when everyone else took it on, I realized the punkest thing I could do was acquire manners, cultivate being a gentleman, being kind, and writing thank you notes.

JLO: I'm the least confrontational person you will ever meet, but my looks keep getting me cast as the villain, beheading people, drawing blood.

HR: Before you ever met, you shared a formative cultural passion.

DL: Both my parents were photographers, so they were always making art in the dark, plus my dad was also a big fan of vintage and camp film. So he would show me Hitchcock films when I was ten years old. And *Barbarella*. Stanley Kubrick's *The Shining* tweaked my visual perspective for the rest of my life. I also found great comfort in watching the films of Danny Kaye, because he was redheaded and striking, but masculine in a great and likable way.

JLO: In the movies I could find incredible women who looked like me: Natalie Wood in *Rebel Without a Cause*, Elizabeth Taylor in *Giant*. These dark-haired goddesses blew my mind and gave me hope. Oh, and I did love black-and-white horror films, though I watched them from behind the couch.

HR: You don't make feature films—not yet—but whether taking in your window installations, set or costume designs, even your candles and product packaging have an undeniably cinematic aura to them.

DL: I used to say I was shooting for the Disneyland effect, but now I refer to it as a calculated hallucination. I want to capture someone's attention unexpectedly. I imagine an investment banker trucking down Fifth Avenue on his phone glances at my window, and suddenly it's as if he's caught shrapnel in his eye. He is completely distracted, and for a second he starts to dream. When he does, then I have done my job.

HR: Usually people attracted to the dark side of romance prefer to remain underground, perhaps to maintain their edge. But you don't feel that way.

DL: Dark or happy, everyone loves romantic stories. And I want these stories of passion for people, for objects, for art, to be seen by the masses. That's why working on the show *Queen of the Night* was so extraordinary. The creative director, Giovanna Battaglia, gave me the opportunity to work with amazing talents like Jennifer Rubell, Randy Weiner, Simon Hammerstein, and Thom Browne to devise a three-dimensional world where I could explore the five senses of luxury. The current technology is ever-present and valuable, but it can drive people into their homes.

I have dark hair. Love a red lip. I avoid the sun. I look gothic and harsh. Not very beachy.

However, if you can take that technology and use it to create visual splendor, people will come out to experience it.

HR: Where did you meet and why were you instantly attracted to each other?

JLO: A roller rink. Mind you, we are both terrible skaters. But Douglas has an incredible gift. He can transform the world around him and make everything so hypnotically beautiful. The first time I ever saw one of his windows, I hit my head on the glass because I was trying to get closer.

DL: Jodi's heart is extraordinary. It's encompassing, funny, astounding, and mysterious. I've been given this incredible gift because being with her makes it possible for me to share beauty as we see it with others.

HR: What's your favorite film?
DL: *Rear Window*; it fits.
JLO: *Young Frankenstein*; it fits.

HR: What's the one thing you will never wear?
DL: Anything neon.
JLO: White denim. The color of cellulite should never be that close to your ass.

HR: Where's the one place you would never go?
DL: A Republican rally.
JLO: Ikea.

Edward Bess

I HAVE COATS THAT WEIGH MORE THAN HIM. IF THE TWO OF YOU WERE WALKING UP RIVERSIDE DRIVE AS THE WEST SIDE HAWK WAS ABOUT TO BLAST ITS BITTER WIND, YOU MIGHT BE TEMPTED TO TETHER HIM AS A PRECAUTION. CHARMING, GENTLE, AND UNNERVINGLY PRETTY, HIS CASCADING HAIR ESCAPED FROM A PANTENE AD. BUT, POUND FOR POUND, THIS LITHE MAKEUP MAVERICK IS THE BALLSIEST SOUL IN THIS BOOK, POSSESSING A FEARLESSNESS ONE WOULD NORMALLY ATTRIBUTE TO ROB GRONKOWSKI, THE TIGHT END OF THE BOSTON PATRIOTS. HIS STORY IS A SERIES OF FORTUITOUS EVENTS CONSISTENTLY DRIVEN BY JAW DROPPING NERVE; LIVING ALONE AS A TEENAGER IN NEW YORK, DEVISING HIS "LIP WARDROBE" WITH NO PRIOR TRAINING, COLD CALLING BERGDORF GOODMAN EXECS, THEN...ACTUALLY, IT'S MORE ASTONISHING WHEN HE TELLS IT.

HAL RUBENSTEIN: How did you get your parents to let you live by yourself in New York City at fifteen?

EDWARD BESS: The first time I visited, my eyes turned into saucers. The glitz and glamour was everything I ever dreamed of magnified to the max. I figured my way in was studying theater, so I auditioned for the "*Fame* school" (Fiorello H. LaGuardia High School for the Performing Arts) and got in. The amazing part was not that my parents let me move, but that I arrived in town a few days before September 11th, 2001 and they let me stay.

HR: So did you decide you were "gonna live forever" and "learn how to fly"?

EB: I didn't get the chance. I got stopped on the street in tenth grade and was asked to consider modeling. It was another rabbit hole I couldn't wait to slide down. So between sixteen and eighteen I was surrounded by photographers, stylists, designers, makeup artists, and it was my idea of heaven. Though I was exposed to beauty as a child thanks to my sisters and my mom and I had lots of opinions, I was never an artist. Now I got to see the application of product, the types of beauty I was attracted to, and observe women's desires and vulnerabilities.

HR: And what intrigued you most?

EB: Two things. First, women wore too much makeup. I believed almost every woman I saw would look better paring it down. But my big revelation was that lip color could immediately change the face—it was like shimmying into the right dress—but that the shade of lipstick that let a woman look her best was likely to be the one closest to her natural lip color. Bright or dramatic options might snare the most attention, but people were noting the color, not the

49

woman, whereas a woman would get the most positive response when she chose an enhanced version of her own lips.

HR: But what do you do with a revelation when you don't have the skills or cash to act on it?

EB: Fools rush in. I was so naïve; I didn't know what a company was. But I found a chemist who would help me formulate my ideas, and he had a friend who was in industrial design who could produce the little black box I envisioned.

HR: But why did they take you on? No offense, but you were nineteen and untrained, to use a kind word.

EB: I guess I didn't know what I didn't know, but they sensed I was on a mission and trusted my assurance and my natural instincts for color. They never patronized me. I asked for ten lipsticks and five glosses, and that's what I got.

HR: With nowhere to take it! So, how does the Lip Wardrobe wind up debuting in Bergdorf Goodman?

EB: I knew that Ed Burstell was in charge of cosmetics only because I read it in *Women's Wear Daily*. I figured I might able to get past his gatekeepers and get his direct line if I called the store after hours, typing his name into the automated directory, and it worked. The next day I called him and got an appointment.

HR: And he said yes, just like that?

EB: I was very determined on the phone, though when I showed up, his first thought was that I was cutting class. But I think he was surprised to see my passion, and he admitted the product was stellar. After three meetings I got a little stand in the store, except I immediately sensed no one could sell my product, but me. So, every day I stood beside my lip colors and stopped woman after woman. Initially, they were shocked by my bravado, but once they realized I

had created the product they'd turned around. Maybe they initially bought out of pity or duty, the way you buy Girl Scout Cookies, but almost every one of them came back. We sold out pretty quickly.

HR: And now?

EB: QVC, Forty Five Ten, launching my Black Sea line, face cream, eye cream, hair products, brows—well, that will require a little more thought—but I don't want to stop. If I can keep proving that makeup has the power to transform, not by hiding or making you feel like you are in costume, but by maximizing each woman's natural beauty, then I can make thousands of them, maybe every one of them, happy. I would like that.

If I can keep proving that makeup has the power to transform, not by hiding or making you feel like you are in costume, but by maximizing each woman's natural beauty, then I can make thousands of them—maybe every one of them—happy. I would like that.

Erin Wasson

AN ALL-AMERICAN BEAUTY WHO TAKES NO SHIT, A MICHAEL KORS RUNWAY STAPLE YOU'RE NOT LIKELY TO FIND HANGING OUT IN PALM BEACH OR GSTAAD, SHE IS FUNNY, DIRECT, FEARLESS, BEWITCHING, THINKS PATTI SMITH IS A GODDESS, HAS A FINE JEWELRY LINE CRAFTED TO REFERENCE ALL THESE TRAITS, AND IF YOU THINK THE WAY SHE DOES—AND SHE LEAVES LITTLE REASON NOT TO DO SO—HER STUFF MAY LOOK NEARLY AS GOOD ON YOU.

HAL RUBENSTEIN: Is it a myth that every model has built-in style?

ERIN WASSON: Oh, come on. If I see one more girl off the runway in a black moto jacket, white T- shirt, jeans, and combat boots, I'm going to scream. No, it's hardly a given. For that matter, how many people in fashion wear a can't-be-bothered uniform?

HR: But you're not one of them.

EW: I was lucky to start my career in 2000 at a precipice of change in fashion, midway between what it was and what it was becoming. I came in right after the Brazilian glamazons, along with the Belgian girls like Delphine and Hannalore, who were all quirky with an odd, mysterious beauty. I had a shaved head, but at that time the industry made room for those of us with strong wills and a desire to be free and eccentric, so I was able to say, "Take it or leave it."

HR: Why did they take it?

EW: There was a lot less pretense then. Instead, there was magic and naughtiness in the air, a focus on personality, individuality, and it allowed some poetry to happen. For example, why does everyone think James Dean is the most stylish dude who ever lived? Every day he wore the same thing those models that I just trashed wear. But it was the way Dean walked down the street. Off a runway, it's not about the clothes. It's about attitude, spirit. What's more attractive than casual confidence?

HR: So what changed this cultivation of self that allowed you to flourish?

EW: Social media changed everything. When I started, nobody was documenting what was going on. If someone wore something special, it was for the rush of it. Now dressing up is contrived. It's a practiced craziness. So much effort is expended on second-guessing what others might find intriguing. Clothes have become a tool to be recognized.

HR: Does it work?

EW: If you consider having a million Instagram followers a barometer of success. I don't have it on my phone. I let someone else do it for me and save my energy for more creative aspects. I do have empathy for younger models these days. They are taking social media classes, learning algorithms, instead of using their imaginations. Andy Warhol said, "You have to be willing to get happy about nothing." Spending time alone with oneself and getting off on it is how the creativity happens.

HR: Why did you choose jewelry as a current outlet for your creativity?

EW: I made costume jewelry for a decade. At the time it made sense because I was aiming at a younger girl and a price point that jibed with the clothes I was doing, or when I was working with Alexander Wang or Zadig & Voltaire. But while I was creating something that girl could afford, I was having a hard time staying passionate about something that's fleeting. I was missing the romanticism of the permanent.

HR: How is that romance built into fine jewelry?

EW: A subliminal narrative of your life is revealed through your fine jewelry. I have a lot of tattoos, and in a way tattoos and jewelry are similar because they often mark poignant moments, and both will stay with you forever. Even if you do get rid of fine jewelry, you will do it in the most beautiful way by passing it along to someone else. It allows the story to continue, and storytelling is the best way any of us communicate and reveal our personality and our heart.

HR: Do you have pieces you never take off?

EW: Regardless of the story I am telling with my clothes, jewelry is punctuation, my exclamation points and my quotation marks. When I go to work on a shoot and I have to take my pieces off, my body is gasping for them at the end of the day. I need my shining idiosyncrasies to make my body whole again.

HR: What else feeds your outlook?

EW: Where I live. I was in Williamsburg for seventeen years when it was a Polish community and cool, and then it got "cool" and weird. Then I found my way to Venice, and then it got discovered, "cool" and weird. So I bought in Ojai. But the change in a year has been disturbing. Luckily, I have Dallas.

HR: Dallas is cool?

EW: Yes! It used to be my dirty little secret because so many people have a false image about it. Like the women in Dallas are so smart and eccentric and cultured. They know about art and style, about having a good time, giving back, and finding your own perspective. These are the women who have supported Brian and Forty Five Ten over the years. They seek new things instead of coveting what others have that they've posted on Instagram. The more we go against the grain, the more we become different people. Don't you want to know people who are different?

Kelly Wearstler

TALENT IS ESSENTIAL, BUT TIMING IS EVERYTHING, AND YOU RARELY CAN PLAN YOUR GOOD FORTUNE. IN THE MID-90S, CALIFORNIA WAS HAVING A MOMENT, BOUTIQUE HOTELS WERE REDEFINING TRAVEL, AND MODERNISM DESPERATELY NEEDED TO FIND ITS COMFORT ZONE. ENTER, THE RIGHT GIRL IN THE RIGHT PLACE WITH EXACTLY THE RIGHT FLOOR PLANS, DESIGNS, AND TASTE LEVEL TO BRILLIANTLY HARNESS ALL THREE TRENDS, FUSING THEIR COMPLEMENTARY APPEAL WITH A DYNAMIC ARRAY OF STRONG MASCULINE SILHOUETTES, CONFIGURED IN FEMININE PROPORTIONS, THEN PAINTED, PAPERED, LACQUERED, AND UPHOLSTERED IN COLORS THAT MADE YOU GLAD YOU WALKED INTO THE ROOM. HER WORK HAS SINCE BECOME A TEMPLATE COPIED REPEATEDLY AND OFTEN SHAMELESSLY BY OTHERS, BUT ITS MAINSTREAM ACCEPTANCE HAS ONLY EXPANDED HER REACH, INCREASED HER INFLUENCE, AND CONFIRMED HER APPEAL. HAPPINESS CAN BE A CHAIR YOU WANT TO SIT ON.

HAL RUBENSTEIN: When was the first time you were able to fully exercise your instincts in shaping an environment?

KELLY WEARSTLER: When I moved into my first apartment in L.A. I went to the flea markets every weekend. I never missed going because there used to be such treasures to be found. I'd say 30 percent of my apartment was flea market finds.

HR: Did you want to show the place off immediately, or were you hoping to keep it your Fortress of Solitude?

KW: Well, the fates kind of took over. I actually am quite shy in private, but I was proud of what I had done, so I persuaded a friend to ask a photographer he knew if he'd shoot it. The photographer was Grey Crawford, who not only said yes but really liked the place and his shoot so much he sent the pictures off to Marian McEvoy at *Elle Décor*, who embraced it, published it, and suddenly I was in business.

HR: Did those found treasures lay the foundation for your own designs?

KW: I certainly incorporated those pieces, but with each new client and each new inspiration, my perspective changes. I like to keep things challenging. Even if I love a fabric, I'll use it for a few projects, then move on. Otherwise, you're not giving anyone anything original. And your talent starts to feel like work.

HR: With such a distinctive profile, people are constantly knocking you off. Do you stamp your feet and reclaim turf or toss that concept over your shoulder and move on?

KW: Imitation is both a compliment and an irritation. But I can't give it a lot of thought since there are so many new things to try and no reason to get locked into one aesthetic.

HR: What's the biggest change in design since you started your business?

KW: Access, for one. Technology has made everything available: clothes, appliances, furniture, accessories, art. There really is no excuse for anyone to be badly dressed anymore, to not have the most efficient gadgets, to not be inspired by something new and different. The choices keep coming. And then, the more educated you become, the more interesting choices you make.

HR: But your new horizons can't only be found on new apps and websites?

KW: I have a huge personal library. I explore the Tate in London, the Musée des Arts Décoratifs in Paris, LACMA in L.A. It's essential to reference history and the past masters of design as well as emerging artists. It's the hardest thing for junior designers to learn, incorporating the past into their present and future.

HR: Which are your signature pieces you can't live without?

KW: My Dichotomy table (the base has two large hands on either end, one holding up a glass tabletop, the other with fingers pressed onto the floor), the Leona stool (a low, conical diner-style seat hoisted by three short Munchkinesque "legs"), and my Soufflé chair (an enveloping cocoon, curved in almost every direction, often covered in multifolded leather). Each is eccentric yet distinctive, and completely functional.

HR: What's the most glorious piece of clothing you've ever worn?

KW: My son had a bar mitzvah this year, and I wanted a cool jacket. I know that Libertine has all these amazing patch jackets, so I had them make one that featured key moments of Oliver's life on it, from his hockey number, to his favorite color, his birth date. It was glorious because it was meaningful to me and to him.

HL: What fashion is most in line with your sensibility?

KW: I would say Gucci because Alessandro Michele's designs are deliberately haphazard and yet have great rhythm, and his use of color and pattern is genius. I also love J.W. Anderson's stuff including his work for Loewe. It's quirky and sexy and has unexpected details. I like things that aren't precious and are slightly off. And like my interior designs, I want to wear old with new. I love hats, crazy fucked up shoes, and accessories that are odd in scale. There is energy in the unexpected.

HR: What famous residence would you love to get your hands on?

KW: The White House. Everything is so stodgy there.

Patrick McDonald

"I RAN OUT OF THE HOUSE SO FAST, I BARELY DID ANYTHING. NOT EVEN MY EYEBROWS," HE SAYS SIGHING IN MOCK EXASPERATION. "LOOK AT ME IN A CHAMBRAY SHIRT, YET. I LOOK ALMOST NORMAL." UH…NO. AND THAT'S THE BEAUTY PART OF THIS MAN. FOR AS LONG AS I HAVE KNOW HIM (WHEN WE MET, THE OWNER OF FORTY FIVE TEN WAS IN ELEMENTARY SCHOOL) HE HAS NEVER LOOKED LIKE ANYONE ELSE. HIS PORTRAIT SHOULD BE IN THE DICTIONARY ALONGSIDE THE WORD "DANDY." NOT THE MEANING THAT DENOTES A "FOP," HOWEVER, BUT THE ONE THAT DEFINES THE ADJECTIVE AS "A MAN ABOUT TOWN." LIKE AMERICAN EXPRESS, HE HAS BEEN EVERYWHERE YOU WANT TO BE AND A FEW PLACES YOU PROBABLY DON'T HAVE THE GUTS TO GO. THERE ARE TRIALS TO DRESSING AS A DANDY. YOUR PRESENCE STOKES THE IRE OF THE INSECURE. BUT IN THE END, THAT'S THEIR SHIT TO DEAL WITH. BUT THE JOY OF DRESSING LIKE YOU ARE ALWAYS READY FOR A PARTY IS THAT YOU WILL USUALLY FIND ONE, OR EVEN BETTER, IT WILL COME TO YOU. AND THOUGH THE MORNING AFTER CAN SOMETIMES BE ROUGH, THE STORIES, TALES, AND EXPERIENCES THE DANDY CAN RECALL AND REGALE MAKE HIS CONVERSATION MORE SPARKLING THAN A MAGNUM OF CRISTAL.

I remember I was only ten when my family drove to San Francisco to see *Mame* at the Curran Theater. The moment I saw all these flamboyant men in ruffled shirts and ascots, I knew I wanted to dress just like them.

HAL RUBENSTEIN: A dandy without penciled eyebrows is like Cher out of fishnets.

PATRICK MCDONALD: I'll have you know I owned those brows long before Boy George and Culture Club. In fact, I sported a full face of makeup when I was still living at home in San Luis Obispo. I remember I was only ten when my family drove to San Francisco to see *Mame* at the Curran Theater. The moment I saw all these flamboyant men in ruffled shirts and ascots, I knew I wanted to dress just like them.

HR: But what or who was the catalyst for the eyebrows?

PM: When I came to New York in '78, my first job was working at Fiorucci alongside Joey Arias. Together we went to a matinee of the *Rocky Horror Picture Show*, and I took one look at Tim Curry eyes (as Dr. Frank-N-Furter) and said, "I can do this! This is me!" But what really sealed the deal was the guidance I received from the greatest makeup artist of all time.

HR: Who was that?

PM: I met Elizabeth Taylor through her hairstylist José Eber in the early '80s. We were getting dolled up at her house in LA for a Halloween party at Studio One— the gay club in West Hollywood— when Elizabeth said, "Sit down. I'm going to do your makeup." Not only did she show me how to perfectly shape my brows, she gave me very Cleopatraesque eyes. I had on a punk wig, and at the end of the night I gave it to her as a thank you. She later wore it to a Prince concert.

HR: A dandy's wardrobe is quite the financial strain on a salesperson's salary, even with your Fiorucci discount.

PM: I was fortunate to be a small trust fund baby so I could afford clothes while I worked there, and by the time that stream ran dry, I'd been hired first by Clovis Ruffin and then Fabrice, so I didn't have to deny myself that Thierry Mugler big-shouldered white jacket and the paper-zipped jumpsuit to wear under my Norma Kamali sleeping bag coat. I could be as outrageous as I liked, working at a fashion house by day and playing at clubs like 54 by night, because my life offered me back-to-back safety zones. It became a little harder when stepping out of that bubble.

HR: How so?

PM: People were intimidated. They asked me to wash everything off and tone down the prints before they'd hire me. When I wouldn't change anything, doors closed. So I returned to fashion's sheltering embrace, first at Barneys, then at John Anthony.

HR: With our culture finally celebrating diversity and acceptance, is it easier today to stand out as you've always done?

PM: Not really, because fashion is too focused on following

the leader now and dressing for momentary effect as opposed to developing and evolving one's personal style. Note that we're not talking about drag, which is everywhere. But apart from that, we're witnessing a rash of outrageous dressing devoted solely to documenting special one-off events like Fashion Week or the Met Ball. I got dressed up because it was Tuesday and I felt like wearing something unexpected. I don't know if there really is a market anymore for my brand of passionate self-expression. Nor does it help that deliberate artifice doesn't resonate on a smartphone. It looks smaller than life.

HR: But don't collections like Gucci push the limits in your direction?

PM: Hey, I'm all for the resurgence of the male peacock, though I'd go a little easy on the chiffon. Give me a ruffle shirt and a palazzo pajama pant anytime. Unfortunately, have you actually encountered anyone wearing any of it on the street? It's not like I'm suddenly seeing new variations of myself coming and going. Confining this aesthetic to posts turns them into fabulous costumes. For me, it's daywear. Maybe as I get a little older I will do what John Anthony did and stick to wearing black. I know it will be a seismic adjustment and maddeningly monotonous, but it will go great with my eyebrows and beauty mark.

Nº 10

Lynn Yaeger

Essay by Lynn Yaeger

YOU MIGHT THINK IT IS A DESPERATE BID FOR ATTENTION, OR A SORT OF SILENT SARTORIAL PROTEST AGAINST COMMONLY HELD NOTIONS OF "ATTRACTIVENESS," OR EVEN A HEDGE AGAINST GROWING OLDER. AND PERHAPS IT IS ALL THOSE THINGS, BUT THERE IS SOMETHING ELSE TOO. WHEN IT COMES TO WEARING WHAT CAN BE SUMMED UP WITH THE WORDS "ECCENTRIC FASHION" I WOULD ARGUE THAT THE IMPULSE COMES FROM A VERY DEEP PLACE, AN AREA BURIED DEEP IN THE PSYCHE THAT MR. FREUD HIMSELF—A GUY WHO WAS LOYAL TO STARCHED COLLARS AND TWEEDY OVERCOATS—WOULD HAVE A HARD TIME UNRAVELING.

In my own case, sticking as I have for years to a signature style that relies heavily on big puffy dresses, tutus, and spangled ballet flats—the sort of things a wildly overgrown six-year-old might wear to a birthday party—the penchant made itself known early. I remember coming home from the third grade and telling Mommy that I wasn't wearing pants ever again (this may have had something to do with my chubby physique) and, on another occasion, begging her to buy me what I called an "angel blouse"—a white empire-waisted thing that my mother, appalled, thought resembled a maternity garment.

Let other girls hang around the Massapequa pizza parlor in hot pants and midriff tops! Lynnie always had some kind of baggy frock on, even at Jones Beach. Of course, though the fundamentals remained eternal, there were shifts over the decades—while every one else was in big-shouldered Norma Kamalis, I was deep in my Clara Bow-Louise Brooks period, drifting through a series of starter jobs (I got fired a lot, but that's another story) flaunting 1920s beaded frocks and bee-stung, kewpie-doll lips.

Sometimes a particular designer stoked my fantasies. When Romeo Gigli burst upon the scene, I saved every penny—no easy task—for his velvet Poiret-inspired cloaks; when Japanese designers like Comme des Garçons suggested I could swath myself in a shredded black shroud, I thought I had already died and gone to fashion heaven. (Who knew polyester could be this chic?)

Then again, sometimes my admittedly "strong" look doesn't elicit quite the reaction I intend. Who among you, dear readers, has been mistaken for Raggedy Ann, in my case more than once? The first time was on the crosstown bus, and as it happened, it was Halloween,

so can you blame a preschooler for jumping to conclusions? The second time was far more recently—a few months ago, in Cleveland, at the Republican National Convention, when a state trooper bellowed, "Who are you supposed to be? Raggedy Ann?" (I didn't argue with him; he had a gun.)

Surprised to learn that I was at the RNC? Don't be—believe it or not, looks can be powerfully deceiving. I was covering the convention for Vogue.com, because who says a lady in a tutu can't also be a deeply serious person? Think about it—after all, isn't it our birthright as Americans to dress as funny as we like, and live by our own rules in this great country?

Think about it—after all, isn't it our birthright as Americans to dress as funny as we like, and live by our own rules in this great country?

ACKNOWLEDGMENTS

This book could not have been written without the creative genius
of Ruven Afanador and his team, the thoughtful words of our friend Hal
Rubenstein, the trust of our amazing subjects, and the patience of everyone
at Assouline. My personal thanks to Prosper Assouline for believing in the
project, and his incomparable eye on the final edit.

—Brian Bolke on behalf of Forty Five Ten